John
Lewis

John Lewis

COURAGE *in* ACTION

MATT DOEDEN

LERNER PUBLICATIONS ◆ MINNEAPOLIS

Lerner Publications Company
A division of Lerner Publishing Group, Inc.
241 First Avenue North
Minneapolis, MN USA 55401

For reading levels and more information, look up this title at www.lernerbooks.com.

The images in this book are used with the permission of: The Photo Access/Alamy Stock Photo, p. 2; AP Photo, pp. 6, 29; Library of Congress, pp. 8, 13 (LC-DIG-fsac-1a33894), 14 (LC-J694-255), 25 (LC-USZ6-1847); Paul Schutzer/The LIFE Premium Collection/Getty Images, p. 9; Bettmann/Getty Images, pp. 10, 12, 15, 16; New York Times Co./Getty Images, p. 17; Kreeder13/ Wikimedia Commons (CC BY-SA 4.0), p. 19; The Peep Holes/Wikimedia Commons (PD), p. 20; Everett Collection Inc/Alamy Stock Photo, p. 22; AP Photo/Nashville Police Department, p. 23; Everett Collection Historical/Alamy Stock Photo, pp. 24, 31; Afro American Newspapers/Gado/ Getty Images, p. 26; AP Photo/Ric Feild, p. 34; AP Photo/Linda Schaeffer, p. 35; White House Photo/Alamy Stock Photo, p. 37; Albert L. Ortega/Getty Images, p. 39; AP Photo/Ron Harris, p. 40.

Front cover: Jeff Hutchens/Getty Images.

Main body text set in Rotis Serif Std 55 Regular 13.5/17. Typeface provided by Adobe Systems.

Library of Congress Cataloging-in-Publication Data

Names: Doeden, Matt, author.
Title: John Lewis: Courage in Action / written by Matt Doeden.
Description: Minneapolis, MN : Lerner Publications Company, 2018. | Series: Gateway
  biographies | Includes bibliographical references and index. | Audience: Age 9–14. |
  Audience: Grade 4–6
Identifiers: LCCN 2017026119| ISBN 9781541512382 (lb) | ISBN 9781541512399 (eb pdf)
Subjects: LCSH: Lewis, John, 1940 February 21–Juvenile literature. | Legislators–United States–
  Biography–Juvenile literature. | African American legislators–Biography–Juvenile literature.
  | United States. Congress. House–Biography–Juvenile literature. | Civil rights workers–United
  States–Biography–Juvenile literature. | Civil rights movements–Southern States–History–
  20th century–Juvenile literature. | African Americans–Civil rights–Southern States–History–
  20th century–Juvenile literature. | Southern States–Race relations–Juvenile literature.
Classification: LCC E840.8.L43 D64 2018 | DDC 328.73/092 [B]–dc23

LC record available at https://lccn.loc.gov/2017026119

Manufactured in the United States of America
1-43994-34003-8/1/2017

CONTENTS

The Deep South 11

A New Perspective. 15

Stepping into Adulthood 18

Committing to the Cause 21

Marching On 24

A New Life 30

Entering Public Service. 32

Conscience of the Congress. 36

Challenging the White House 38

Important Dates 42
Source Notes 44
Selected Bibliography 46
Further Reading 47
Index 48

John Lewis, 1963

Violence was coming. Twenty-one-year-old John Lewis was sure of it. It was the spring of 1961, and racism was widespread in the United States, especially in the South. In many states there were laws in place to segregate, or separate, black people and white people. This meant they could not attend the same schools, use the same bathrooms, or sit in the same waiting rooms. But in 1960, the US Supreme Court—the highest court in the United States—decided that segregation in train and bus stations around the country was no longer legal. African Americans traveling across the country would be allowed to use the same bathrooms, waiting rooms, and restaurants as white travelers.

However, many state governments were not enforcing this decision in areas across the country. So Lewis and twelve others, known as the Freedom Riders, went on a journey to test these laws. Lewis had no doubt that at some point on their journey, the group would face violent opposition. He just didn't know when.

A Greyhound bus station in South Carolina

On May 4, the thirteen riders had boarded buses in Washington, DC, and headed south. They planned to reach New Orleans, Louisiana, on May 17. The Freedom Riders—seven of them black and six white—planned to ignore signs for separate bathrooms and waiting rooms along the way.

Lewis understood that by taking this stand, he was risking his life. He knew he might die on this trip. Many in the group even wrote wills before boarding the buses in Washington, DC, to explain their wishes in the event of their deaths. Yet the group traveled through Virginia and North Carolina without serious incident. On May 9, they arrived in Rock Hill, South Carolina. That's where everything changed.

Lewis approached the waiting areas at the Rock Hill Greyhound terminal. One waiting room was reserved for white passengers. A second was marked Colored. Lewis fixed his gaze on the room for white passengers.

As he approached the door, several young white men watched. "[They] were leaning by the doorjamb to the waiting room," Lewis later wrote. "They wore leather jackets, had those ducktail haircuts."

Two of the men stepped between him and the door. They told him to use the other room. Lewis didn't move.

That's when it happened. The violent outburst came so

A group of Freedom Riders approaches a waiting room and restaurant marked for white customers.

Lewis and fellow Freedom Rider James Zwerg stand together after being attacked at a bus station in Montgomery, Alabama, on May 20, 1961.

quickly that Lewis had no time to react. "The next thing I knew, a fist smashed the right side of my head," he wrote. "Then another hit me square in the face. As I fell to the floor I could feel feet kicking me hard in the sides. I could taste blood in my mouth."

The vicious beating went on as people watched. Eventually, a police officer stepped in to break it up. Lewis was bleeding and in pain. Yet even as more police officers arrived, he refused to press charges against his attacker.

His anger was not with any one person but with the system that allowed blacks to be seen as second-class citizens.

After facing such an assault, Lewis could have called it quits. But he didn't. He continued to protest and fight for people of different races to have equal rights. And he continued to pay the price, facing more violence over the coming weeks and years. Yet Lewis kept fighting. The fight by Lewis and many others for equality and an end to segregation and discrimination lasted many years and became known as the civil rights movement. Lewis rose to the forefront of the movement and continued working for equality for more than fifty years.

The Deep South

John Robert Lewis was born in Troy, Alabama, on February 21, 1940. He was the third child of Eddie and Willie Mae Lewis. They were sharecroppers, or tenant farmers. They worked on land owned by another farmer. They received part of the money the farmer earned when he sold his crops. Alabama was in the heart of the Deep South, a region where white and black people mostly did not mix. Many whites saw black people as less than human.

John attended segregated schools. His family went to all-black churches. His neighbors and friends were black. As a child, he had almost no contact with white people at all. But he knew racism existed. John was a bright

Students listen to their teacher at an all-black school in Virginia in 1947.

and curious child. He enjoyed school and was a good student. He especially loved reading. Growing up, John never traveled far from his home. So books opened doors to a wider world. But John was not allowed to go to the library. He wanted more than anything to browse the shelves of the Troy Public Library, but black people were banned from it. Lewis could only imagine the inside of the building. The injustice of a public library being off-limits frustrated him.

During growing season, John worked with his parents and siblings in the fields. The family spent long, hard days picking cotton. At the end of the day, they'd sell what they'd picked—often around 400 pounds (181 kg) of cotton—for about $1.40. John hated that his family worked so hard for so little pay and that society in Alabama at the time left them no way to improve their situation. He later wrote, "As soon as I was old enough to make sense of the world around me, I could see that there was no way a person could get ahead as a tenant farmer."

John complained to his parents. He had read about black figures such as Booker T. Washington and George Washington Carver. Through their stories, John realized that black people could make a difference in the world. They could be more than sharecroppers who scraped by day after day. But every time he questioned the fairness

A family works in a field of rented land in Georgia in 1941.

Booker T. Washington was born into slavery. But he was determined to get an education and a better life. He later founded a school for black students.

of laws that seemed to hold down black people, his mother would make him stop. She understood what racism meant, and she knew how some whites would treat a black person who spoke out against it. Nothing John said or did could change their situation. And so life went on. John kept going to the fields with his parents, all of them hoping they would earn enough money to get by.

In 1951 John took a trip north to New York with his uncle. There he saw that black people were treated differently than they were in the South. They didn't have to be afraid of offending a white person. They could move around where they wanted, not restricted by Whites Only signs. Racism still existed, but it didn't hang over everything a black person did. After seeing life in the North, his Alabama home never felt quite the same to him again. He dreamed of a life different from that of his parents.

A New Perspective

The year 1954 marked a big change in the practice of segregation. The Supreme Court heard a case called *Brown v. Board of Education of Topeka.* This was a lawsuit against schools in the United States that did not allow black students to attend.

Three US attorneys who argued against segregation in the *Brown v. Board of Education* case stand in front of the US Supreme Court Building.

The lawsuit said that segregation in schools kept some children from getting a good education. In its decision, the court declared that schools had to allow both black and white students. John was thrilled to read accounts of the decision in newspapers. He imagined that his world was about to change drastically.

It didn't. Despite the court's decision, segregation remained alive and well in the South. If anything, things got worse. The ruling, along with the growing civil rights movement, fueled more hatred than ever among some whites. A hate group called the Ku Klux Klan (KKK) grew rapidly in the South. KKK members harassed and assaulted black people who they thought had stepped out of their roles as second-class citizens.

Students size each other up in a newly desegregated classroom in Virginia in 1954.

In 1955 John turned on the family's radio and heard a booming voice giving a sermon. The message was a call to action and a plea for black people everywhere to come together and demand equal rights. John was captivated. Only after the sermon was complete did he learn the name of the young minister who had delivered it: Martin Luther King Jr.

"It seemed like Martin Luther King Jr. was speaking directly to me," John later said. "[He was] saying 'John Lewis, you too can do something. You can make a contribution.'"

John didn't know it yet, but around this time, King was becoming the face of the civil rights movement. His powerful manner of speech touched millions. All over the country, from north to south, people were joining the cause. John set out to read everything he could about King. He found something he had been seeking for a long time—a voice that put into words his own feelings about racism in the United States. King became John's role model. The teenager wanted to fight by King's side. He wanted to make white people listen and change.

Over the next few years, John watched as the civil rights movement grew. He felt pride as protesters staged a bus boycott, refusing to ride on city buses and demanding respect for black riders in nearby Montgomery, Alabama. He was filled with horror when black teenager Emmett Till was brutally beaten and killed for innocently flirting with a white woman. Emmett's murder hit John hard. John was fifteen at the time, just a year older than Emmett. "That could have been me," he wrote. "I felt like a fool. . . . It didn't seem that the American principles of justice and equality I read about in my beat-up civics book at school mattered."

Martin Luther King Jr., 1955

John grew angry with the system that allowed people to be so mistreated. More and more, he was filled with a sense of purpose. Things needed to change, and he wanted to help change them.

Stepping into Adulthood

In 1957 Lewis graduated from high school. It was time for him to leave Alabama to begin making a difference in the world. A deeply religious young man, Lewis planned to become a minister. Lewis had hoped to follow in King's footsteps by attending Morehouse College in Atlanta, Georgia. But the tuition at Morehouse was far more than Lewis could afford. So Lewis went to the American Baptist Theological Seminary (ABTS) in Nashville, Tennessee. The school didn't charge any tuition. Instead, students worked on campus to pay for their education.

At first, the seventeen-year-old felt very out of place. Most of the students at ABTS were much older than him. Many had traveled the world, while he had barely been outside of Alabama. He was shy and self-conscious.

But Lewis was itching to start making a difference. He thought about Troy State, a university near his hometown that still didn't allow black students to attend, and he decided to take a stand. Lewis sent in an application to the school.

Months passed, and he didn't hear anything back. It was clear the university was ignoring him. So Lewis wrote a letter to King, describing his situation. To his amazement, King wanted to meet with him. In the summer of 1958, Lewis boarded a bus to Montgomery. There, in the basement of First Baptist Church, the eighteen-year-old finally got to meet his hero. King was interested in Lewis's quest to desegregate Troy State. He offered to do everything he could do to help, but Lewis had to get his parents' permission.

Lewis felt ready to take on the system, but his parents were less confident. They asked him not to go through with it. They knew he could be hurt, and they worried that Lewis's father might lose his job. Lewis desperately wanted his parents' blessing, but he understood their concerns. So he made the hard choice to back down. His first real stand against segregation was over before it began.

Lewis returned to ABTS. He became more and more involved in the civil rights movement, which was dedicated to protesting peacefully, without engaging in violence.

These ideas were inspired by Mohandas Gandhi, a leader in India who had used nonviolent methods to campaign for India's independence from Britain. Together

Lewis's application to whites-only Troy University in Troy, Alabama, was ignored by administrators.

with a group of other students from Nashville, Lewis learned more about nonviolence. In 1959 they planned to stage sit-ins to protest segregation. Lewis's first big protest was at a department store called Harveys. Lewis and a group of others—white and black—sat at a whites-only lunch counter. Their protest gained little reaction. But other groups began planning their own sit-ins in other department stores. The sit-ins grew larger and larger. At just eighteen years old, Lewis was following his dreams and fighting for equal rights.

American Baptist Theological Seminary, the school Lewis attended after high school, was later renamed American Baptist College and continues to educate students in Nashville.

Committing to the Cause

As the calendar turned to 1960, change was in the air. The civil rights movement was fully under way, and Lewis was determined to be at the heart of it.

Lewis and others were planning their biggest sit-in yet. It would range across several department stores in Nashville. On February 13, Lewis was part of a group that sat at a lunch counter in a Woolworth's store.

The store employees said little as the protesters sat. Instead, they simply put up a Closed sign at the counter and turned out the lights. Hours passed, and the protesters continued to sit in the dark. Some white Woolworth's customers taunted them. They shouted racist comments and told the protesters to go home. But Lewis and his fellow protesters didn't budge. At about 6 p.m., they quietly went home.

The protesters went back several times. Each morning they marched by the hundreds to fill lunch counters throughout the city. A week after the protest began, the tempers of those who opposed the protest were rising, yet there still had been no violence. The police warned protesters that they would be arrested, but that didn't stop them.

On Saturday, February 27, tempers finally boiled over. Lewis was with a group at Woolworth's when several young white men attacked them. Lewis was pushed from his stool, but he didn't fight back. He just got up and sat back down again. Throughout the city, TV cameras rolled as black protesters were attacked. When the police finally

A group of protesters sits at a lunch counter in Nashville in 1960.

arrived, it wasn't to arrest the young white males for assault. It was to arrest the protesters—Lewis included.

As Lewis was led away by police, he felt something change. "Now I knew," he wrote. "Now I had crossed over, I had stepped through the door into total, unquestioning commitment. This wasn't just about that moment or that day. This was about forever."

After spending about six hours in jail, Lewis and the others were released. Their protest had made national headlines. People across the country were talking about it. The protesters had done exactly what they'd set out to do.

The lunch counter protest served as Lewis's true introduction to the civil rights movement. Its success had helped him see how he could make a difference.

But his parents disapproved of his actions. To them, getting arrested was something criminals did. They couldn't understand why Lewis was proud of his arrest.

But Lewis was not discouraged. A year later, he was one of the original thirteen Freedom Riders who opposed segregation in bus stations. Despite violent opposition and several beatings—including Lewis being knocked unconscious in Montgomery, Alabama—the protesters carried on. The rides stretched through the summer, and so did the violence. But the Freedom Riders helped raise awareness for civil rights and give civil rights issues a place in American politics.

Photos from John Lewis's arrest during the sit-ins in Nashville

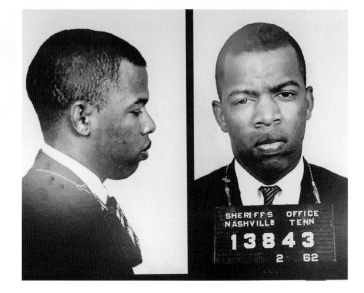

Marching On

In 1963 Lewis became the chairman of the Student Nonviolent Coordinating Committee (SNCC), an organization that helped students organize protests and gave young people a voice in the civil rights movement. At the age of twenty-three, he was the youngest member of a group called the Big Six—the leaders of the nation's six major civil rights organizations.

That same year, about three hundred thousand Americans, including both black and white citizens, traveled from every US state to Washington, DC, to demand equal rights and freedom for all Americans. Those who participated in the event, known as the March on Washington, wanted to make sure lawmakers knew about the challenges that many Americans still faced because of racism and discrimination. The March on Washington was a memorable moment. Lewis was one of the speakers. He ended his speech with a passionate call to action:

> We will not stop. . . . But we will march with the spirit of love and with the spirit of dignity that we have shown here today. By the force of our demands, our determination, and our numbers, we shall splinter the segregated South into a thousand pieces and put them together in the image of God and democracy. We must say: "Wake up America! Wake up!" For we cannot stop, and we will not and cannot be patient.

Another Movement

Nonviolence was at the core of the civil rights movement. However, not everyone agreed that nonviolent approaches were effective in every instance when it came to standing up for civil rights. Another movement, which would become known as Black Power, was also growing.

The Black Power movement was closely tied to a group called the Nation of Islam (NOI). The NOI wanted to use violence at times when they believed nonviolent methods were not leading to change in the fight for equal rights. In the 1960s, both movements grew. But a popular leader of the NOI, Malcolm X, left the group in 1963. In 1965 Malcolm X was killed, and another NOI leader, Louis Farrakhan, was widely suspected of ordering the assassination. These events helped to cause a decline in the Black Power movement. By the late 1960s, King's nonviolent methods were back at the heart of the civil rights movement.

King (*center*) and Malcolm X (*right*) stand together before an event in 1964.

King (*front row, second from left*) and other civil rights leaders walk at the front of the March on Washington.

Lewis's speech was one of the highlights of the march. He spoke from the same podium as Martin Luther King Jr., who delivered his famous "I Have a Dream" speech. The march was a success. It played a large role in convincing lawmakers to pass the Civil Rights Act of 1964. This law said that people could no longer be separated in public places because of race. The new law was a victory, but the fight was far from over for Lewis, King, and other activists.

That was never more clear than after the events of Sunday, March 7, 1965. Lewis was leading a march from Selma, Alabama, to Montgomery to demand equal voting rights for all races. While black people were allowed to vote in elections, those who tried often faced discrimination. Election officials might tell black voters that they had filled out forms incorrectly or that they couldn't read well enough to vote. The protesters wanted to end this discrimination. That Sunday around six hundred protesters gathered at a church in Selma. From there, they marched silently, two by two, through downtown. The line of marchers stretched for several blocks.

As the marchers reached the Edmund Pettus Bridge leading out of Selma, they met a force of 150 armed state troopers, sheriff's deputies, and others. The troopers ordered the marchers to turn around. They gave the protesters two minutes to do so.

Lewis makes his speech at the 1963 March on Washington.

But Lewis wasn't about to turn around. Even if he'd wanted to, it didn't seem possible. The marchers stretched back for blocks. And he wouldn't march forward, toward the troops, to provoke violence. All he could do was stay where he was. He and the others knelt and prayed.

One minute and five seconds later, the police advanced. They had clubs, tear gas, and whips. A large man carrying a club towered over Lewis. The man raised his arm and bashed his club into Lewis's head. Lewis crumpled to the ground as the scene burst into chaos.

Troopers threw tear gas at the protesters. Lewis and others near the front began to cough and choke as white onlookers cheered. At that moment, Lewis believed he was going to die.

"I really thought it was my last protest, my last march," he said. "I thought I saw death, and I thought, 'It's okay, it's all right—I am doing what I am supposed to do.'"

The marchers turned to flee, pressing through the mass of bodies behind them. Lewis managed to pick himself up off the ground and join the retreat. The troopers followed the protesters more than a mile back to a church, continuing to brutally beat anyone who strayed.

The day came to be known as Bloody Sunday. Many marchers were severely injured, including Lewis, who had a fractured skull. The brutal attack became international news. People around the country began to support civil rights activists. When a second march was planned, President Lyndon Johnson sent the National Guard to Selma to protect the marchers.

Progress was slow and bloody, but the movement was gaining momentum. The days of segregation were quickly coming to an end, and Lewis was a big part of the reason why.

Lewis falls to the ground as a state trooper with a club stands over him during the March 7 Selma-to-Montgomery march.

A New Life

In 1965 President Lyndon Johnson signed the Voting Rights Act into law. This law prohibited racial discrimination by election officials. It marked a major turning point in the civil rights movement. The gains, slow at first, were coming more rapidly. But the years of fighting had taken their toll on Lewis. He was exhausted. Meanwhile, the SNCC was growing more and more divided. The lure of the Black Power movement was taking hold among some younger members. SNCC members argued about the organization's direction. In 1966 Lewis was replaced as chairman.

At the age of twenty-six, Lewis left the SNCC. Civil rights remained important to him, but he no longer wanted to have a leadership role. It was time to move on to the next phase in his life.

It wouldn't be easy. "There I was," he wrote, " . . . starting my life over, broke, with no job, no skills, no wife, no children, no place even to call home."

Lewis thought about going back to school. But he had no money. First, he needed a job. It didn't take him long to find one. He was offered a position at Field Foundation, an organization in New York that provided money for groups involved with child welfare and civil rights around the country. With nowhere else to turn, Lewis packed his things and headed north.

Lewis felt lost and alone in New York. After just a year, he took a new job at the Southern Regional Council (SRC). He moved to Atlanta, Georgia, where he felt more

President Lyndon Johnson signs the Voting Rights Act in August 1965.

at home, and he traveled around the South, helping people in poor communities work together to make sure everyone had food, jobs, and shelter.

In the South, the next chapter in his life truly began. At a New Year's Eve party in 1967, he met Lillian Miles. Miles, a librarian, was a supporter of the civil rights movement and had long admired Lewis from afar. "I was attracted to him before I knew him," she later said. "Every day and every night on the news was something about what was happening in the civil rights movement, so I felt like I knew him."

The pair started dating. Lewis, despite his years at the forefront of the civil rights movement, still had a quiet personality. Miles, meanwhile, was bold and unafraid to speak her mind. It was a perfect match.

Over the next year, the couple grew closer. It was a difficult year. On April 4, 1968, Martin Luther King Jr. was shot and killed. It was a crushing blow to Lewis.

Two months later, Lewis lost another friend when Bobby Kennedy, who had been running for president, was shot. Miles was by Lewis's side during those dark times.

On December 21, Lewis and Miles married. About three hundred people gathered for the ceremony. Martin Luther King Jr.'s father performed the service. The next year, the couple bought a home in Atlanta. In 1976 they adopted a son, two-month-old John-Miles Lewis. Lewis was thrilled to be a father. He later said that he fell in love with John-Miles the first time he saw him.

Entering Public Service

In the late 1960s and early 1970s, Lewis became more and more involved in politics. He believed that political action was the way to bring change to the United States. He took a position with the Voter Education Project (VEP), where he reached out to black voters to teach them about politics and help them register to vote. Lewis also worked on and supported the election campaigns of both African Americans and whites. By late 1976, people were asking him when he was going to run for office himself.

Lewis was torn. To run, he would have to quit his job with the VEP. His wife was working, but with a baby at home, the idea of being unemployed was frightening. In 1977 a congressman from the Atlanta area left his position in the House of Representatives. Voters would elect a new representative that spring. Lewis decided it was time. He left his job and entered the race.

Lewis lost that election, but in 1981, he was ready to give politics another shot. This time, he ran for a place on the Atlanta City Council, and this time, he won. He served from 1982 to 1986, fighting to support the city's poorest neighborhoods.

In 1986 Lewis again ran for the US Congress. The first task was to win the nomination of the Democratic Party. Lewis ran against Julian Bond, a friend and respected state senator. Many considered Bond an overwhelming favorite to win the nomination. The media—both local and national—covered the race. It was a battle between two former civil rights leaders. Bond seemed to have all the advantages. He was an experienced politician. He was an eloquent speaker who had gained national celebrity, appearing on the popular late-night show *Saturday Night Live*. His campaign had more experienced staff, more money, and a better understanding of how to run an election campaign. Many of Lewis's friends told him to drop out of the race. He couldn't hope to beat Bond. Even Lewis later admitted that his chances looked bleak.

Yet the more people told Lewis that he couldn't win, the more convinced he became to do just that. He reached out to communities that had been largely ignored in the past—Jewish voters, gay voters, and Latinos. And he also appealed to white voters, winning them over with his humble beginnings and his work ethic. Lewis walked the streets of Atlanta, greeting voters and winning support, one person at a time.

Lewis casts his ballot in the 1986 election. His wife and son stand beside him.

Bond's huge lead in the polls slowly began to shrink. Yet Bond still appeared firmly in control. Lewis watched the election results on TV. The afternoon turned into evening, and Bond was still ahead. Around midnight, a reporter interviewed Lewis. When the interview was finished, he was still behind.

The final areas to report results were mainly white neighborhoods. And they voted overwhelmingly in favor of Lewis. Lewis and his team watched as Bond's lead dwindled and then disappeared. Instead of giving a speech saying he had lost the election, Lewis was headed to a victory celebration. It was a stunning upset.

Next, Lewis had to run against the Republican nominee, Portia Scott. He had no trouble winning that election. He was running in one of the most Democratic districts in the country. Lewis defeated Scott with 75 percent of the vote. He was headed to the US Congress.

Lewis (*left*) and his wife lead supporters in a march celebrating his 1986 campaign victory.

Conscience of the Congress

On January 3, 1987, Lewis was sworn in as a member of the One Hundredth US Congress—and he has held the position ever since. He joined a growing number of black lawmakers who made up the Congressional Black Caucus. This group works to support the interests of black voters on a wide range of issues.

Voting rights remained an issue close to Lewis's heart. He continued to reach out to voters of all races, encouraging them to vote in local, state, and federal elections. Lewis fought for change to health-care laws, and he supported laws designed to end poverty and improve education. Lewis's record of fighting for his ideals has earned him the unofficial title Conscience of the Congress.

Lewis has faced some criticism while in office. Republicans have accused him of being unwilling to compromise on issues. In 1991 he opposed the United States' entrance into the Gulf War (1990–1991), though many lawmakers and citizens supported the action. In 2001 he did not attend the inauguration of President George W. Bush. Lewis claimed that Bush was not the true president because of controversy surrounding the election results in Florida. Critics say that Lewis often uses exaggerated statements to attack opponents. Lewis has compared some of his opponents to Nazis, a hateful political power that ruled Germany during World War II, or to George Wallace, the racist governor of Alabama during part of the civil rights movement.

In 2007 Lewis supported Hillary Clinton in her campaign to earn the presidential nomination for the Democratic Party. But he also watched with interest as up-and-coming Senator Barack Obama gained support in the party. In February 2008, Lewis officially said he supported Obama for the presidency: "I think the candidacy of Senator Obama represents the beginning of a new movement in American political history that began in the hearts and minds of the people of this nation," Lewis said. "And I want to be on the side of the people."

Lewis watched with pride as Obama won the Democratic nomination and then the presidency. Just four decades after Lewis had marched to secure voting rights for all people, the nation had its first black president.

President Obama hugs Lewis during an event in 2015.

Challenging the White House

Lewis remained one of President Obama's biggest supporters throughout the next eight years. He was in favor of many of Obama's policies, including health-care reform and greater gun control.

Lewis watched as the 2016 presidential election unfolded. Hillary Clinton earned the Democratic Party's nomination, while Donald Trump won the Republican bid. Despite polls that indicated that Clinton would win, Trump came away with the victory. Trump had many critics, but few were more vocal than Lewis. Lewis led a boycott of Trump's inauguration. He accused Trump and Russia of working together to damage Clinton's campaign. He called Trump's presidency illegitimate and said Russia had been involved in the election.

Trump fired back. The president taunted Lewis with a series of tweets on Twitter. He said of Lewis, "All talk, talk, talk—no action or results. Sad!"

Trump's words struck many as odd, considering Lewis's long record of activism and public service. The public feud made national headlines. Democrats and many Republicans supported Lewis. Nebraska senator Ben Sasse—a Republican—noted, "John Lewis and his 'talk' have changed the world."

The feud fueled a renewed public interest in race relations and in Lewis himself. Sales of his biography skyrocketed, selling out on Amazon.com.

Through it all, Lewis continues to push for social change and greater equality and opportunity for all.

Author John Lewis

Ever since he was a child, Lewis has loved books. So it's no great surprise that he went on to become an author as well as a politician. In 1998 he published an award-winning biography, *Walking with the Wind: A Memoir of the Movement.* In 2012 he published *Across That Bridge: Life Lessons and a Vision for Change.*

In 2013 Lewis tried something new. As a kid, he'd been inspired by a comic

Lewis displays two of his graphic novels at Comic-Con International in 2015.

book about Martin Luther King Jr. He hoped to have a similar impact on young people. So he started a three-book graphic novel series, titled *March.* The trilogy told the story of the civil rights movement through Lewis's eyes.

That was his fight when he stepped aboard a bus as one of the first Freedom Riders. It was his fight as he led marchers out of Selma. And even as he approaches eighty years of age, it remains his fight that he wages in the halls of Congress.

Lewis attends the 2017 Atlanta March for Social Justice and Women, a peaceful demonstration held in support of the rights of women and underrepresented communities in the United States.

"In the final analysis, we are one people, one family, one house—not just the house of black and white, but the house of the South, the house of America," Lewis said. "We can move ahead, we can move forward, we can create a multiracial community, a truly democratic society. I think we're on our way there. There may be some setbacks. But we are going to get there. We have to be hopeful. Never give up, never give in, keep moving on."

IMPORTANT DATES

1940 John Robert Lewis is born in Troy, Alabama, on February 21.

1955 He hears Martin Luther King Jr. speak over the radio. The speech inspires him to become part of the civil rights movement.

1957 Lewis graduates from high school and enters American Baptist Theological Seminary.

1965 He leads a march out of Selma, Alabama. The marchers are confronted and attacked in an event known as Bloody Sunday.

1968 Martin Luther King Jr. is killed on April 4. Lewis marries Lillian Miles on December 21.

1976 John and Lillian adopt a son, John-Miles.

1977	Lewis runs for a seat in the US House of Representatives but is defeated.
1981	He enters public service with his election to the Atlanta City Council.
1987	He is sworn in as a member of the One Hundredth Congress.
1991	He opposes the US entrance into the Gulf War.
2008	He endorses Barack Obama for president. Obama wins the election, becoming the first African American president.
2012	Lillian Miles Lewis dies.
2017	Lewis leads a boycott of the inauguration of newly elected president Donald Trump. This sets off a public feud with the incoming president.

SOURCE NOTES

9   John Lewis and Michael D'Orso, *Walking with the Wind: A Memoir of the Movement* (New York: Simon & Schuster, 1998), 142.

10 Ibid.

13 Ibid., 24.

16 Joshua Berlinger, "Rep. John Lewis Goes Back to His Roots," *CNN.com*, June 23, 2016, http://www.cnn.com/2016/06/23/politics/john-lewis-sit-ins/.

17 Lewis and D'Orso, *Walking with the Wind*, 57.

22 Ibid., 108.

24 John Lewis, "Speech at the March on Washington," Voices of Democracy, accessed April 19, 2017, http://voicesofdemocracy.umd.edu/lewis-speech-at-the-march-on-washington-speech-text/.

28 Jon Meacham, "G&G Interview: Congressman John Lewis," *Garden & Gun*, February/March 2015, http://gardenandgun.com/articles/gg-interview-congressman-john-lewis.

30 Lewis and D'Orso, *Walking with the Wind*, 373.

31 Michelle E. Shaw, "Lillian Miles Lewis, 73: Wife, Adviser of U.S. Rep. John Lewis," *Atlanta Journal Constitution*, December 31, 2012, http://www.ajc.com/news/local-obituaries/lillian-miles-lewis-wife-adviser-rep-john-lewis/xVff5GSZZAiolGRhhj765O/.

37 Jeff Zelney, "Black Leader Changes Endorsement to Obama," *New York Times*, February 28, 2008, http://www.nytimes.com/2008/02/28/us/politics/28lewis.html.

38 Cleve R. Wootson Jr., "In Feud with John Lewis, Donald Trump Attacked 'One of the Most Respected People in America,'" *Washington Post*, January 15, 2017, https://www .washingtonpost.com/news/the-fix/wp/2017/01/15/in-feud-with -john-lewis-donald-trump-attacked-one-of-the-most-respected -people-in-america/.

38 Ibid.

41 Meacham, "G&G Interview."

SELECTED BIBLIOGRAPHY

"John Lewis." Profile. *Finding Your Roots. PBS.org.* Accessed May 1, 2017. http://www.pbs.org/weta/finding-your-roots /profiles/john-lewis.

Lewis, John. "Speech at the March on Washington." Voices of Democracy. Accessed April 19, 2017. http://voicesofdemocracy.umd .edu/lewis-speech-at-the-march-on-washington-speech-text/.

Lewis, John, and Michael D'Orso. *Walking with the Wind: A Memoir of the Movement.* New York: Simon & Schuster, 1998.

Marill, Michele Cohen. "The Last Dreamer." *Atlanta Magazine*, August 1, 2003. http://www.atlantamagazine.com/civilrights/john-lewis/.

Meacham, Jon. "G&G Interview: Congressman John Lewis." *Garden & Gun*, February/March 2015. http://gardenandgun.com/articles /gg-interview-congressman-john-lewis.

Zelney, Jeff. "Black Leader Changes Endorsement to Obama." *New York Times*, February 28, 2008. http://www.nytimes.com/2008/02/28/us /politics/28lewis.html.

FURTHER READING

BOOKS

Boehme, Gerry. *John Lewis and Desegregation.* New York: Cavendish Square, 2017. Learn more about Lewis's role in the civil rights movement, the protests he helped to organize, and the opposition he faced.

Braun, Eric. *Taking Action for Civil and Political Rights.* Minneapolis: Lerner Publications, 2017. The fight for civil rights can come in a variety of forms. Learn more about how activists have battled for the rights of others and how you can take up the fight.

Outcalt, Todd. *All about Martin Luther King, Jr.* Indianapolis: Blue River, 2016. Read about Martin Luther King Jr. in this illustrated biography about one of the most influential members of the civil rights movement.

WEBSITES

Civil Rights for Kids—Ducksters
http://www.ducksters.com/history/civil_rights/
Learn more in this broad review of civil rights, the history of civil rights activism, and some of history's most famous civil rights champions.

Civil Rights Movement—PBS.org
http://www.pbs.org/black-culture/explore/civil-rights-movement /#.WQekcRMrIdU
Articles, videos, and images tell the story of the fight for civil rights in the United States.

Congressman John Lewis
https://johnlewis.house.gov/
Lewis's official congressional page includes the latest news on him, his stances on legislation, contact information, and more.

INDEX

American Baptist Theological
    Seminary (ABTS), 18–20
Atlanta, GA, 18, 30, 32–33

Bloody Sunday, 28
Bond, Julian, 33–34
*Brown v. Board of Education of
    Topeka,* 15
Bush, George W., 36

Civil Rights Act of 1964, 26
Clinton, Hillary, 37–38

Democratic Party, 33, 35, 37–38

Freedom Riders, 7–8, 23, 40

Gandhi, Mohandas, 19

Johnson, Lyndon, 28, 30

King, Martin Luther, Jr., 16, 18–20,
    25–26, 31–32, 39
Ku Klux Klan (KKK), 15

March on Washington, 24
Miles, Lillian, 31–32
Montgomery, AL, 17, 19, 23, 26

Nashville, TN, 18, 20–21

Obama, Barack, 37–38

Republican Party, 35–36, 38

Selma, AL, 26–28, 40
sit-in, 20–21
Southern Regional Council (SRC), 30
Student Nonviolent Coordinating
    Committee (SNCC), 24, 30

Troy, AL, 11
Trump, Donald, 38

US Congress, 33, 35–36, 40

Voter Education Project (VEP), 32
Voting Rights Act, 30

Washington, DC, 8–9, 24
Woolworth's, 21